BLESS YOURSELF CHRONICLES

10 Steps to Breathe Life into Your Redesign

Keona T. Ellerbe

BLESS YOURSELF CHRONICLES: 10 STEPS TO BREATHE LIFE INTO YOUR REDESIGN. Copyright

Cover Design: Graphic Artist ALS Graphic Designs | www.als-graphic-designs.com

©2016 by Keona Ellerbe. All rights reserved. Printed in the United States of America. No part of this book may be used or reproduced in any manner whatsoever without written permission except in the case of brief quotations embodied in critical articles and reviews. For more information, address Redesign of U, LLC Publishers.

Redesign of U, LLC books may be purchased for educational, business, or sales promotional use. For information, please e-mail redesignofu@gmail.com or visit www.redesignofu.com.

FIRST EDITION

Library of Congress Cataloging-in-Publication Data has been applied for.

ISBN: 978-0-692-78450-1

All scripture references in this book are from the King James Version which is public domain.

Table of Content
Breathe ~ Redesign

Introduction
    Are you ready to Redesign your life?

Breathe 1
    Find Yourself   04

Breathe 2
    Forgive Yourself   11

Breathe 3
    Love Yourself   15

Breathe 4
    Be Yourself   21

Breathe 5
    Do Not Hide Yourself   27

Breathe 6
    Do Not Abuse Yourself   34

Breathe 7
    Make an Agreement   40

Breathe 8
    Never Settle   45

Breathe 9
    Believe   53

Breathe 10
    Closing the Door   58

Breathe Bonus

Conclusion

Epilogue

Acknowledgements

I would first like to give ALL thanks and honor to my Heavenly Father. Without Him placing this gift in me I would not have been able to birth this book. Lord, without your tests and trials, I would not be able to help and serve your individuals. I am humbly thankful that you can speak through me.

Next, I have to thank my mother, Marguerite Jefferson, and father, Lee Watson, for raising a headstrong child that would not take NO for an answer and for showing me unconditional love. I thank my grandparents (Luellen & Bertha Bushrod and Pattie Watson) for praying for me without ceasing. I know that their fervent prayers are what covered me through the years. I wish that you all were here to see all that I have become and see God's gift shining brightly, but I have come to realize that I needed you more in spirit than actually being on this earth. You all speak to me often and I draw strength from your unwavering love.

I have to thank my husband Kelton Ellerbe for all that we have gone through together. Despite it all, we are still standing together, locked arms ready to take on the world. We know that we are stronger together than being apart. You have lit a fire in me that the world is getting ready to watch burn. There must have been a reason I married a firefighter because you know how to extinguish a fire and to also how to keep it burning. Thank you.

Last, but not least, my four handsome princes (Kylin, Keeon, Kelton II and Kendrick). Without you, Mommy would still have six pack abs. No, honestly a mother could not ask for anything more. You each are totally different, but I love each of you the same.

As I am writing this book for you, the reader, I am also writing it for myself. Just because I wrote this book does not mean that I still do not have to bless myself daily. Your mind is the hardest thing to control and because of that you have to be careful about what you allow in your eye gate and your ear gate. Just one thing you see or hear can throw off all the work you have done to keep your mind under control. Tell yourself: I AM in control of me. Through my thoughts and actions, I WILL BLESS MYSELF AND NOT CURSE MYSELF. *Proverbs 18:21a KJV, "Death and life are in the power of the tongue."* Simply put, watch what you say about yourself.

This book is dedicated to all those who are ready to redesign themselves.

Genesis 1:27

"So God created man in his [own] image, in the image of God created he him; male and female created he them."

In this passage, God created (designed) you in his likeness. Take a moment and describe how you see yourself.

_____
_____
_____
_____
_____

Repeat this- If God created me this way, then I AM DESIGNED IN HIS LIKENESS AND I AM G-O-O-D Good.

Introduction

When I take a quick glance over the 34 years that God has blessed me to be on this earth. I began to wonder how my life would have been different if my parents would have remained married. What would have happened if I only saw the rich neighborhoods and not having experienced the poverty stricken areas? What would have happened if I never had my heart broken? Life is filled with "what ifs," but the blessing is in knowing that those things that I was exposed to have shaped me into the AWESOME person that I am today. I know that you are wondering "WOW she called herself AWESOME," that is right. I AM who I say I AM. Before we move any further. What do you say about you? Go ahead, write it_____. It may take you a minute or you may not know at all and that is okay. This is the reason for this book. I am going to show you how to unlock your true self.

In this book you will find areas that will cause you to self-evaluate and that is just to assist you in breathing life into yourself. When you go through life, certain situations cause you to feel like you have been in a fight. And you have, you have been in a fight with yourself. And if you have ever had the wind knocked out of you, it is not a good feeling, but what you must do is fill your lungs back up with air so that you can

BREATHE again. I have designed these 10 steps to help you breathe life into yourself.

So go ahead and take time to write a statement about yourself. For example, here is mine: I AM an intelligent, strong, beautiful, courageous and a God fearing woman. I will NOT let a "No" from anyone cause me to lose focus on my goals and dreams.

_____
_____
_____
_____
_____

We will refer to this statement periodically throughout the book and you will have the option to either change your statement or keep it the same. But you will begin to learn more and more about yourself that you did not know existed and that is okay. These steps are meant to dig into some places that you have covered, buried and hidden from yourself.

Genesis 2:7

"And the LORD God formed man of the dust of the ground, and breathed into his nostrils the breath of life; and man became a living soul."

The Design

Breathe 1

FIND YOURSELF

Once you find yourself, everything else will fall into place.

On a scale of 1-10 (10 being the highest), how well do you think you know yourself?

One of the things that I knew nothing about was myself. I did not know what made me happy. I did not know my purpose. I was wandering through life wondering why I was not happy and it was because I did not know who I was. It was not until I began to ask my Heavenly Father very specific questions about myself to realize my purpose. My purpose was simple: to share my story on how I found myself and help others figure out where they lost themselves. **This is the redesign!**

I am a wife, mother, daughter, and a friend. While being all of these things, I began to focus on making others happy and not truly finding out what mattered most to me and why I was placed on this earth. It would frustrate me when someone would ask what do you like or what makes you happy. I could never answer those simple questions because I did not know myself well enough to answer them. I would somehow maneuver around it and begin to talk about something else. I was extremely good at swerving, but it was not a good trait because it kept me from truly answering the difficult question.

So I ask you: what do you know about yourself? What is your purpose in life? God has placed a gift in each one of us and He loves to see those gifts in operation. Why? Because the gift he gave you is not for you, it is for the benefit of others. My gift is to serve and help you so that you can learn what makes you special.

Here are four suggestions that will assist you in starting this redesign process:

1. **Find a mentor**- Before you begin to look for a mentor, ask yourself this question: What do you want this person to help you accomplish? After you have determined what that is, you can then begin your search. A mentor will help you to determine your strengths and weaknesses. They should help you to create goals, milestones and deliverables. Your mentor should be a great listener that never criticizes you, but you have to be open for constructive feedback. Through this feedback you will be able to determine why you keep getting stuck in the same place.

2. **Get organized**- The Bible says it best, *1 Corinthians 14:40, "Let all things be done decently and in order."* Have you ever been looking for something and you know you have it, but it is not where it is supposed to be? When things are not organized in your life, it throws everything out of balance. Begin to balance your personal, financial, and spiritual life. Start with the small things first. For example, organize the 'stuff' drawer in your kitchen. (Yeah, I know that you have one because I have one too.) Determine when you are going to sit down to develop a financial spreadsheet on what you spend a month compared to what you bring in. And last, but certainly not the least, set aside prayer time. Yes, I know some of say that I talk to God in the car on my way to work. That is great; but He wants to have your undivided, uninterrupted attention. He wants to talk to you concerning you.

3. **Find an accountability partner**- *Proverbs 27:17, "Iron sharpeneth iron; so a man sharpeneth the countenance of his friend."* Accountability is the ability and willingness to give an account to someone else of your actions and motives. Find someone that is trustworthy, that will challenge you, but not condemn you. This person should know where you are weak and help you to overcome that struggle. Some individuals have more

than one accountability partner depending on where they need help. I know who I can go to when I want the real and unfiltered support and I know who I can go to when I want to be coddled. These individuals keep me grounded when I am ready to fly off the handle, but you MUST trust your accountability partner and not go against the advice that they give you. If you are still going to do what you want to do, then this relationship will not work for you or your accountability partner.

4. **Be prepared to take a leap of faith**- *James 2:20, "But wilt thou know, O vain man, that faith without works is dead?"* Be prepared to make yourself uncomfortable. Being stretched and taken outside of your comfort is going to cause you to grow. I promise you, that once you begin to stretch yourself, you will never go back to that place where you were. Trust the process of finding what makes you, uniquely yourself. Do not be alarmed when you begin to lose friends, it is okay. Individuals who do not know who they are or what they want will begin to question why you are acting different. It is okay, your difference is part of your growth and redesign. Those who stick by you during this process are those with whom you need to be acquainted. The

others, you needed to lose anyway because they are not going to fit into your new circle.

Breathe Evaluation

What do you say about you?

_____
_____
_____

How well do you know yourself after reading this first chapter?

_____
_____
_____

Do you have a mentor/coach? If so, who are they and why did you chose them?

_____
_____
_____

Is your life organized? If not, what date are you giving yourself to complete this?

_____
_____
_____

Do you have an accountability partner(s)? Who are they? What are they holding you accountable to do?

_____
_____
_____

What makes you uncomfortable? How will you begin to push yourself out of your comfort zone?

_____
_____
_____

You have just began your journey in finding you. How do you feel?

_____
_____
_____

Proverbs 3:5-6

"Trust in the LORD with all thine heart; and lean not unto thine own understanding. In all thy ways acknowledge him, and he shall direct thy paths."

Trust the Process

Breathe 2

FORGIVE YOURSELF

Forgive yourself- Stop looking for others to forgive you. Instead, forgive yourself. You cannot fix what is already done. Move on.

Psalms 103:12, "As far as the east is from the west, so far hath he removed our transgressions from us."

Have you ever felt like you keep reliving the same unfortunate circumstances? Or you have someone that keeps reminding you of what you have done or said in the past? Have you ever wanted to ask them "are you still stuck there?" Well, guess what? You can. If your Heavenly Father can forgive you for what you have done, then do not think man or woman can keep putting you on trial for something that has already been forgiven, but first you have to forgive yourself.

Your book has more chapters. Turn the page…

Give yourself a break. No one is perfect and as part of life, things happen. You may not always do things the correct way and that is okay, but God willing you have the ability to do it over. The key is to learn from your mistakes, recognize what went wrong and avoid repeating the same mistakes. Now, do not get me wrong, sometimes you will trip and fall over that same thing again: it is okay, you may not always get it right on the first try. Just remember that these failures do not make you a bad person.

Adapt a new mindset.
Romans 12:2, "And be not conformed to this world: but be ye transformed by the renewing of your mind, that ye may prove what is that good, and acceptable, and perfect, will of God." You are more than your past mistakes; you are worth it.

Stop feeling bad about yourself. Stop taking yourself through the guilt trip. Guess what? It is now in the past. Now what are you going to do? How are you going to move forward? God is full of grace and mercy. Let Him guide you through this process.

Breathe Evaluation

I want to forgive _____ for _____ _____ _____

I choose to release my feelings of _____ _____ _____.

I acknowledge that releasing those feelings will make me feel _____.

I decree and declare today _____ (write the date) that I will forgive myself.

Proverbs 3:1

"My son, forget not my law; but let thine heart keep my commandments."

I Got You

LOVE YOURSELF

Love Yourself – First love yourself, others will come next.

The greatest gift God gave us was his love through the death of his Son Jesus Christ. Through his love, he died for us and that is why it is imperative that you love yourself. Until you begin to love yourself, you will never be able to whole heartedly love anyone else.

Let me be clear, when I say that you must love yourself, I am not referring to being prideful. I am referring to being thankful for the person that God has created and called you to be.

Psalms 139:14 says it best "I will praise thee; for I am fearfully and wonderfully made: marvelous are thy works; and that my soul knoweth right well."

When I look back over my life. I realized that I suffered mentally because I did not know how to love me. Not only did I not know how to love me, it caused my relationships to suffer because I did not know what was best for me and consequently it prevented me from being able to articulate how I deserved to be treated and loved.

Love yourself, if you do not get anything else from this book, this is the key that *unlocks* everything else in your life. You will begin to love the journey that you are creating by learning to love what you like and changing what you dislike. You will begin to learn things about yourself that you had no clue would interest you. And you will begin to make better choices in the individuals you choose to bring to your inner circle. Those individuals who are in that inner circle should be striving towards making a better life for themselves daily. Some individuals will not be compatible with the new you, they need to go. When you did not know how to love yourself, you were likely hanging around individuals that did not know how to love themselves either. And that was okay during that time, but you are now moving in a different direction and you need individuals who will stretch you and assist you in loving you.

While you are going through this process, it is not meant to be easy. You have a lot of things you need to undo in order to get it right. Consider yourself as an onion, you have some layers that need to be peeled back before getting to the good stuff. You will begin having conversations with yourself on what the old you liked, but stay focused on what your new target is and that is learning to love you. You are going to have individuals telling you that you are selfish. You are not. You just do not have time for their foolishness anymore and they do not understand your transformation. Guess what? They do not have to understand because what you are doing is not for them, it is for you.

Here are a few questions you can ask yourself on your journey to loving you:

Do you realize that there is not another person on this earth that was created like you? Why do you think that question is important? Because when God created you, He wanted you to know that you were perfect in His eyes. Everything about you, down to each individual hair follicle was created by Him.

Do you realize that your gift was only given to you? No one can tell you how to do your gift. What are some of your greatest talents and abilities? Think back to when you were completing a task and someone told you that you are great at or should be doing _____. Most often, individuals see your gift in you before you do. It is just something about you when you are operating in your gift and purpose. You light up and the individuals around you are amazed at how you do what you do. That right there is where you will find your pleasure. It will not be a strain to do it, but you will lose sleep (adrenaline pumping) over doing what you love and it will not matter. Once you have found what makes you happy. DO IT! Do not allow anyone to tell you anything different. It may not always be easy, but keep working on it.

God allowed me to take a small glimpse into the things that I was getting ready to do and all I could do was cry. I began to ask Him how am I going to be able to do this? Where will the money come from? What if individuals do not support me? All of these things were racing through my mind, but then that still small voice said "I gave it to you and I will make provisions for you to get it done." All I had to do was trust in Him and know that all things are possible to them that believe. Do you believe? Do you believe that those visions He gave you will come to pass?

Do you realize that God created you in His image? When you look at yourself, what do you see? Go ahead ask yourself. I will wait. It may be helpful to stand in the mirror. For my ladies: have you ever looked at a picture of yourself and you immediately started to critique it? But when someone else looks at the same picture they do not see what you saw. They see an amazing picture. We do it all of the time without even realizing it. We see ourselves one way, while someone else looking at the same picture sees it another way. Why is that? What is causing us to see our flaws, while others do not notice them at all? We are often so hard on ourselves, but we do not realize that we need to love ourselves more because the world and life will do a great job at breaking us down, if we let it. Unlock you and LOVE yourself!

Hebrews 11:1

"Now faith is the substance of things hoped for, the evidence of things not seen."

Your Natural Eyes Can Not See This

Breathe 4

BE YOURSELF

There was only one of you created for a reason, be you.

When you look at yourself in a mirror; what do you see? It amazes me that there are 320 million individuals in the United States and the odds of finding someone with the same fingerprints is 1:320 million. God created a masterpiece when He created you. He was so thrilled when He created you, that He did not want to make another you. So why is it so hard to be ourselves? Why are we not happy with who we were created to be? I am so glad that God only created one of me because I am not sure that the world could handle all of this AWESOMENESS twice.

We are often times constantly looking around at who we are not instead of being satisfied with who we are. What amazes me most about individuals is that they see what is on the outside, but they do not know what that person may be struggling with internally. Have you ever known someone that was going through hell at home, but when they stepped out in public you could never tell? Some individuals are so good at wearing a mask, while others show all of their emotions.

I know all too well about wearing a mask. I was known for holding in 95% and sharing 5%. I did not really want anyone to know what I was going through because I did not want to be judged for my decisions. What I realized is that wearing this mask was detrimental to my psyche. I began to talk to me about me and as I have previously mentioned, that is not good.

Once I took control of who I am, it helped me to become happy being me. You will be amazed at how many individuals in your circle are not happy being themselves.

Let us talk about some ways that can assist you in being the best you that you can be.

The first step is stop comparing yourself with others. Only compare yourself with yourself. Why is this so important? When you begin to compare yourself with someone else you then begin to become someone that you are not. Remember, just because it looks great on the outside, does not mean that who you are trying to compare yourself to is even happy with themselves. Now, I am not saying that if you notice a trait or habit in someone that you would like to possess, that you should not work towards improving yourself in that area. That is all part of development and growth. Certain traits or habits are imperative for you to have as you get older. It is okay to play an adult game of copycat, just as long as you are copying the right cat.

Parable of The Pencil

The Pencil Maker took the pencil aside, just before putting him into the box.

"There are 5 things you need to know," he told the pencil, "Before I send you out into the world. Always remember them and never forget, and you will become the best pencil you can be."

"One: You will be able to do many great things, but only if you allow yourself to be held in someone's hand."

"Two: You will experience a painful sharpening from time to time, but you will need it to become a better pencil."

"Three: You will be able to correct any mistakes you might make."

"Four: The most important part of you will always be what is inside."

"And Five: On every surface you are used on, you must leave your mark. No matter what the condition, you must continue to write."

The pencil understood and promised to remember, and went into the box with purpose in its heart.

Now replacing the place of the pencil with you. Always remember the five instructions and never forget, and you will become the best person you can be.

One: You will be able to do many great things, but only if you allow yourself to be held in God's hand. And allow other human beings to access you for the many gifts you possess.

Two: You will experience a painful sharpening from time to time, by going through various problems in life, but you will need it to become a stronger person.

Three: You will be able to correct any mistakes you might make.

Four: The most important part of you will always be what is on the inside.

And Five: On every surface you walk through, you must leave your mark. No matter what the situation, you must continue to do your duties.

Isaiah 43:1

"But now thus saith the LORD that created thee, O Jacob, and he that formed thee, O Israel, Fear not: for I have redeemed thee, I have called [thee] by thy name; thou [art] mine."

I Am His

Breathe 5

DO NOT HIDE YOUR VOICE

You should never be bullied into silence.

Have you ever temporarily lost your voice due to a cold or maybe from shouting at a concert or sporting event? If you are anything like me, I would start drinking tea with honey and lemon and then I just keep saying "I'll be glad when I get my voice back." Well, the same applies when you do not use your voice, you begin to lose it.

Some individuals hide their voice after a traumatic experience, but the main reason is FEAR. Fear of being vulnerable or opening a door that you are trying to keep closed. Some hide their voice because they believe that what they have to say is not important, but that is far from the truth. Talking is vital to expressing how you feel, sharing your thoughts and conversing with others. It allows you to put words together to create sermons and speeches that inspire and motivate countless individuals. Your voice allows to you agree, disagree and compliment. So why hide that?

Say something even if you think your opinion is not valued. Have you ever been in class or a meeting and they get to the Q & A section and you want to raise your hand, but you do not want to prolong the conclusion of the meeting or you are afraid that your question is stupid? You get up and leave and all day you are saying to yourself "I should have asked." Or it goes the opposite way; someone asked a question and it was the same question you had? In this instance, here are a few things that happen when no one speaks up:

- It prevents constructive criticism- When you think something is not a good idea, most times there are others who think the same way, but if no one speaks up, it gives the illusion that everyone is okay with the bad idea. Guess what? When the bad idea is implemented, you are upset because you now have to comply with something that you disagree with. If you spoke up, this could have potentially gone another way, but you will never know.
- You need to be noticed- Those individuals who speak up are rated at being more intelligent than those who sit back and just watch. Although, this is not necessarily true, you need to remind individuals that you are a valued member.

Stop saying to yourself that nothing will change even after I express how I feel. First, how do you know until you say it? Secondly, you cannot assume how the receiver will take what you have to say. Assumptions can absolutely ruin your life because you do not know what others are thinking and they for sure do not know what you are trying to say.

Here are a few examples when you MUST speak up:

- When you are being taken advantage of-
- When it compromises your integrity- Never allow someone to back you into a corner; you have a choice. So choose wisely. Anything that can potentially put you in a situation that you may have to answer for down the road, opt out! You may have to lose someone you considered a friend, but a true friend would never put you in a situation like that to begin with.
- When you need apologize- This one can sometimes be a hard pill to swallow, but it is necessary. Have you ever been on the receiving end when someone hurt you and they did not apologize? How did it make you feel? Not great huh? When you are wrong and you know that you are wrong, apologize. It will not only make you feel better, but it also avoid what could potentially turn

into something that could have been avoided. Just remember something that appears to be miniscule to you, could be huge to someone else.

Here are a few tricks that you can use to ensure that you are never bullied into silence:

Increase your faith-

- Read the word- *Romans 10:17 "So then faith cometh by hearing, and hearing by the word of God.".* God's word is the seed that grows your faith. Meditate on His word daily.
- Heed the word- *James 1:22 "But be ye doers of the word, and not hearers only, deceiving your own selves."*
- Test the word- *James 1:2-4, "My brethren, count it all joy when ye fall into divers temptations; Knowing this, that the trying of your faith worketh patience. But let patience have her perfect work, that ye may be perfect and entire, wanting nothing."* Testing the measure of your faith will involve trials and difficulties.

Begin by renewing your mind-

You have to constantly keep your thoughts in check. The mind will begin to wander and before you know it, you are thinking about the wrong things. That is why you must crucify your flesh daily. If you know that your weakness is bread, but you have to drive pass a bakery every day, you might want to pick another route. Can you smell it? The aroma of fresh baked bread seeping through the vents in the car, although you have the windows rolled up. Well, my weakness is shopping, more specifically clothes and shoes. I can go several months without wearing the same shoe and I only wear an outfit once in a season. Someone mentioned that they had been watching me to see if I would repeat an outfit. Needless to say, they were unsuccessful in their research. Because I like to shop, I have to talk to myself while I am in the store to stay focused. If I begin to drift, I might pick up something, but by the time I walk around the store, I have put it down because I know that I did not need it, just wanted it. It took a lot for me to get to this point, once I realized that I control me.

Ask for strength in your prayer time-

Visualize the strength flowing into you. Be specific in your prayer request. You would like strength to_____

_____

_____

_____

_____

_____

_____

Remember, God is always by your side. Have you ever needed someone to talk to and every person you called did not answer? Did you ever think that the person you needed to call on was your Heavenly Father? Sometimes you do not need a conversation with a man or woman, you need "The Man."

Proverbs 28:26

"He that trusteth in his own heart is a fool: but whoso walketh wisely, he shall be delivered."

Ask For Wisdom

Breathe 6

_____

DO NOT ABUSE YOURSELF

Watch what you are saying and thinking about you.

Self-blame amplifies perceived inadequacies, regardless if they are real or imaginary. They paralyze and inhibit forward movement. How do you expect to show love, when you are unable to love yourself first?

Remember, it is not the **enemy** it is your **inner-me**. So, stop allowing you to hold you back.

There have been many days when I had to minister to myself. I may have cried a tear or two and then I had to suck it up and stop feeling bad about my current circumstances. The situations in my life were placed here to grow me, stretch me and take me beyond where I have been. Do you realize the more you ask yourself what you have done to deserve the mistreatment it allows the person who mistreated you to win?

Have you ever been around a person that is just miserable? By the time you finish talking to them you feel miserable too?

Negativity is contagious if you allow it to attach itself to you. Now do not get me wrong, there is a difference between venting and constantly being mad about something. Venting is a good thing; you have to get things off your chest.

Now, there is a difference between taking responsibility and self-blame. I am not saying that you do not have to take responsibility for your actions, because you definitely have to take ownership if it is yours for the taking. We all have made bad choices in life, but you made that choice at the time because you thought it was the best decision. What you have to do is look back at that bad choice(s) and figure out what went wrong. Acknowledge that you made a mistake and apologize to the other parties involved if need be, but do not beat yourself up for something that has already occurred. IT IS OVER!

There was a gentleman that I was dating and he had me believing that his cheating was my fault. And, for a long time, I really thought I did something that caused it. I began to blame myself for why I was hurting and trying to figure out how not to do whatever I did again. It was not until I began to really learn myself that I realized the crap I was being fed was not for me to eat. He cheated because he made a decision to do so. It had absolutely nothing to do with me. That self-blame was making me feel even worse than I already did. Do you see how the mind works? The second you begin to let that thought seep in, it takes over your thoughts and your mind. What if I held on to that foolishness for the rest of my life, thinking I was to blame? How would that negative self-blame end up hurting me and future relationships?

So I ask you: what are you blaming yourself for? What are some things that someone told you was your fault and you did not question it, but you just took ownership of it? Let us take some time to recognize and get rid of everything you are or have blamed yourself for.

Let us start by thinking about an event that you have blamed yourself for.

_____
_____
_____

Why do you blame yourself for this event?

_____
_____
_____

Was this something that was yours to own?

_____

Now after answering the last three questions; if it was not yours, you need to right now LET IT GO! By writing the following: I (your name)_____
will no longer allow myself to be held hostage by holding onto (state what you are blaming yourself for)

_____

_____

_____

and I LET IT GO TODAY!

If on the other hand it was something that was yours to own, say the following:

I made an honest mistake when I

_____

_____

_____

I did the best I could when I

_____

_____

_____

I learned some important lessons when I

_____

_____

_____

I am sorry about

_____

_____

_____

Write the names of the individuals you need to apologize to and be sure to include yourself on this list.

_____

_____

_____

NOW LET IT GO!

While doing this, I hope it helped you to acknowledge any past regrets, right any wrongs and learn from the experience. You are now moving in the right direction to heal and move on. It is time, you deserve it.

Isaiah 41:10

"Fear thou not; for I [am] with thee: be not dismayed; for I [am] thy God: I will strengthen thee; yea, I will help thee; yea, I will uphold thee with the right hand of my righteousness."

Fear and Faith Can Not Co-Exist

Breathe 7

MAKE AN AGREEMENT

It is time to make an agreement with yourself.

Different things motivate different individuals. What is one thing that you would like to accomplish this month? What is stopping you from accomplishing it? Let us make some short-term and long-term goals. The word says in *Habakkuk 2:2b,* *"Write the vision, and make it plain upon tables, that he may run that readeth it."* In order to make an agreement with yourself, I need you to take some time to determine what you want from yourself. What are those things that you would like to accomplish?

Quick question: What are some things you can do to push yourself outside your comfort zone?

_____

_____

_____

Please understand that growth occurs right outside of that zone. You should be growing daily both mentally and spiritually. When was the last time you visited a bookstore to pick up a good book? It amazes me how as grown-ups we think the learning process has stopped because we are no longer in school, but these are the times when you should be reading the most. With all that we encounter on a daily basis, we need to bring our minds back to a neutral place; away from all of the negativity, away from our current environment. Do you realize how much influence our current environment has on the goals that we set for ourselves? We are constantly wondering what the next person is thinking about the business you may want to start of the idea you have. Why are you worrying about what someone else is thinking? Food for thought- The opinion you accept is the lifestyle you will endorse. I love to say what others think are not paying the bills in my house. Guess what? Haters need a job too, so give them something to talk about. If no one is talking about you, you are not working hard enough.

(Sorry I got off topic just that fast…whew, okay reel it back in.)

Let us begin by creating an action plan. What are your long-term goals? What are your short-term goals? What will be the benefit? What is the reward? When you have an action plan, it holds you accountable and keeps you motivated to reach the goal.

_____
_____
_____
_____
_____
_____

These are also things that your mentor or accountability partner can assist you with. Also, if you have never created a vision board, this is a fun way to place some pictures on a board of your goals. You will be amazed at how stimulating this visual is to the brain. Your short-term goals could be as simple at reorganizing your home, creating a new fitness plan or a little more complex like going back to school. Whatever the goal is do not forget to include your completion date(s).

Your long-term goals should be those things you would like to achieve in the next three to five years. These goals should be extremely specific and include measurable and dates for completion.

Let me forewarn you: the minute you set your goals, fear and doubt will come to pay you a visit. You can win!

Cup of Tea

YOU ARE NOT FOR EVERYONE

The world is filled with individuals who, no matter what you do, will point blank, not like you. But it is also filled with those who will love fiercely. They are your individuals. You are not for everyone and that is okay. Talk to the individuals who can hear you. Do not waste your precious time and gifts trying to convince them of your value, they will not ever want what you are selling. Do not convince them to walk alongside you. You will be wasting both your time and theirs and will likely inflict unnecessary wounds, which will take precious time to heal. You are not for them and they are not for you; politely wave them on, and continue along your way. Sharing your path with someone is a sacred gift, do not cheapen this gift by rolling yours in the wrong direction. Keep facing your True North.

Colossians 1:23

"If ye continue in the faith grounded and settled, and be not moved away from the hope of the gospel, which ye have heard, and which was preached to every creature which is under heaven; whereof I Paul am made a minister;"

Unwavering

Breathe 8

NEVER SETTLE

You are always under construction, keep improving.

I have a question: Why do you think you settle for less than you deserve? Here is my observation: You do not believe that you deserve better; you often times think that you have to work with the cards you are dealt or you think that things will eventually just get better and work themselves out. Where are your standards? Those are the things (standards) that you will not waver on, no matter what. When you have standards it is easier to discard thoughts, mistreatment and disrespect because you have settled in your mind that it goes against what you believe in or will tolerate. There will be times in your life when you must self-check, but this is a great opportunity to allow your mentor or accountability partner to assist you during the correction process. There is no need to try to fight this battle alone.

When you set a standard for your life, your goal is to no longer accept anything but what is best for you.

While you are unlocking the best version of you, continue to work on yourself. This can be achieved through personal development. What are you listening to? What are you reading? Your voice should not be the only voice you hear all day long. Why? Because you can bless yourself and curse yourself at the same time.

Standards

When you have a standard for yourself, it will automatically push you into personal development. Your personal development (mental shift) will help you on a daily basis to remain focused on making sure that you are getting a little better every single day. If you would like to become a better person, you need to constantly push yourself to achieve more by your actions, listening better and consistently learning how to outperform the person from the day before. Changing your mindset is one of the most difficult things to do, because you have been conditioned to think a certain way For me, when I set standards for myself, I have to abide by them because I NEVER want to let myself down. The good thing about setting a standard for yourself first, is it makes it easier to set-up standards for other aspects of your life. And guess what, you will begin to attract individuals into your life who also have standards similar for their life. I had a co-worker who was shocked at how well behaved my children were and she asked me what is my secret. I simply stated to her that my husband and I have a standard for our children and the children are aware of what is expected. There are certain things we will and will not tolerate because the standard was set, there was an unspoken language when we were in public as to how they were required to act. Our motto is "it goes down where you act up" so because they understood what that meant, we did not have to reiterate that point, they already knew their parents were crazy. Believe me it is not easy dealing with four boys, but the standard makes it easier. Believe it or not you have standards that are already ingrained in you through your parents, schooling/education, media, society and culture. Each one of those standards have influenced how we look, feel and spend our time. The issue with those ingrained standards cause us to measure ourselves based on the way someone else thought we should be and causes us to become unauthentic. So let us take some time to develop your standard.

Developing a Standard

By now you should have already completed your goals from the previous chapter. If not, take a few minutes to complete them now before beginning on your standards.

Alright, Let us dive into developing your standards.

- What are some characteristics or traits you would like to have?
    - Examples:
        - Honesty- Honesty is more than just simply telling the truth. You have to live the truth. Honesty requires you first being honest with yourself and then others.
        - Forgiveness- Make a conscious effort to let go of resentment and anger.
        - Authentic- Be real and true to yourself.
        - Healthy- Are you happy with the way you look? If yes, how do you plan on maintaining that? If no, how do you plan to change it?

- Are there any changes that you would like to make to your behavior?
    - What are some things that tip you over the edge?
        - Identify them.
        - Write down how you would like to respond to them.

- Write down all of your obstacles.
    - Take a minute to reflect on some of your past failures.
    - Think about how you could have avoided the failure.
    - Now think about how you keep that obstacle from stopping your progress in the future.

- Who are some individuals you respect?
    - Your Religious Leader
    - Parents
    - Spouse
    - Accountability partner

When you begin to think on these things it causes you to have a conscious interrupt and you begin to self-evaluate who you really are compared to the person you want to be. Ultimately, once you have completed the comparison, setting the standard will be easy. *Jeremiah 31:21 says it best, "Set up road signs; put up guideposts. Take note of the highway, the road that you take."*

Are you are wondering where should I set my bar? Begin with the items from the list you have created above and determine which are the most meaningful and non-negotiable. Make a list of things starting with "must." Once you have completed your "I must" list, now create "I would like to" list. For me, once I defined my standards, it ended a lot of my procrastination. I would put things off until the absolute last minute and then I would always say to myself "If I just started earlier I would not have to rush to get it done." I realized that my procrastination was affecting my children because they started waiting until the last minute to get things done as well. The standards that I set helped me to govern the way I organized my time and set priorities.

Once you have set your standards for yourself. You can then begin to work on standards for your family, relationships, work, and career. Just remember that your standards are not set in stone. No, that does not mean you can change them to make this easier. It means that as you begin to work on your personal growth and development, your perspectives will change, for the better. Your standards, just like life will need a re-evaluation and fine-tuning as you blossom and develop. So do not get too attached to them, because as you grow so will your standards.

Let us take a moment and look back on the statement you made about yourself on page 2; would you like to change it? If so, here is a great place to take the mask off and write how you really feel about yourself.

_____
_____
_____
_____
_____

Proverbs 16:9

"A man's heart deviseth his way: but the LORD directeth his steps."

Your Steps are Ordered by God

Breathe 9

BELIEVE

Believing in yourself can be one of the hardest things for you to do especially if you do not have the right support. Many things can prevent you from feeling good about yourself and ultimately believing in you. For example: you could be constantly surrounded by individuals who are negative and negative individuals pull you into a direction that make it hard for you to believe and dream. You must realize that your goldmine is five feet beyond the point when you feel like giving up. When you began to stop fighting for what you want, the devil realizes that you will always stop short the minute a distraction comes into play. I am here to tell you that your dreams are worth fighting for. You will have to push through, kick through and throw somethings around, but just know that it is worth it.

No matter what you are going through, God is only using you.

The minute you begin to put things in motion to overcome your circumstance or accomplish your goals, be prepared to deal with obstacles and distractions. They are purposefully placed there so that when you finally reach the goal you will have a testimony of what you have gone through to get it.

When you are going through the journey, take plenty of notes and talk with your accountability partner. Try to avoid as much negative self-talk as possible because you can talk yourself right out of your blessing and become way off track. Your accountability partner should be just as excited about your journey as you. Remember they are there to keep you focused, provide you with advice and be an ear through your process. If you do not trust the advice of your accountability partner, then that is not the person for you.

When you look at yourself and the decisions that you have made over your life, what do you see? Do you see a person that has done the best he/she could have done at the time? Or, do you see someone that has made so many mistakes and you wished that you could go back in time to fix them? Guess what, regardless of whichever way you answered, there is not anything you can do about the past, except to learn from your past mistakes and make better choices in the future. When I am speaking with clients about how they can improve the way they see themselves, they always start with the negative. Why do we see the negative before the positive? Instead, I prompt them to start with what they have done right and how to perfect those things. Do you realize that if you honed in on those things that you do exceptionally well, the negatives will slowly diminish? How is that? Because you are now mastering the things that you do extremely well and you begin to automatically fix those things that prevent you from mastering you. For example, if you are extremely organized, but you constantly procrastinate, your ability to master being organized will not allow procrastination to seep in. Now let us go the opposite way. Let us say one of your negatives is tardiness. How do you defeat that spirit? Yes, I said spirit. Your spirit will tell you that they never get started on time so it is okay if I arrive late or no one else will be on time. My grandfather was 30 minutes to an hour early in everything that he did. It did not matter if it was a job, dinner or even church. You can count on him being there early no matter what. Have you ever been late for a function and as you sit in traffic, you begin to think if I left 30 minutes earlier? Well, start programming yourself to leave 30 minutes earlier, even if that means you need to set every clock in house to 30 minutes fast. You will begin to notice that you are not as stressed out and individuals that used to see you arrive late, will begin to see you show up on time and wonder what has gotten into you. When you shake-off that spirit, you will begin to notice other spirits that warrant your attention. Remember as I write this book I am preaching to me as well. I am far from perfect and I have come a long way from where I used to be, but I still have to work on myself daily. So do not beat yourself up if you do not get it right away--It is a process. Changing your mindset from 20+ years of programming takes time. Give yourself a hug and tell yourself, "I believe that I am getting better every day."

Luke 21:34

"And take heed to yourselves, lest at any time your hearts be overcharged with surfeiting, and drunkenness, and cares of this life, and so that day come upon unawares."

I'll Hold That

Breathe 10

CLOSING THE DOOR

Now that we have opened some doors that have been closed for some time, what are you prepared to do to properly bring closure to them and delete them from your memory so that you can create new memories? I pray that you have the confidence to know that those things no longer serve you. Those old memories are to be placed in a box and used as a stepping stool to elevate you to the next level. Where is the next level? Where ever you desire to go. Your options are limitless; you are the only person that can set a limit for how far you will go. Remove all self-doubt, fear, anxiety and just jump. You will do one of two things, fly or hit the ground. Either way you are no longer standing in a place of "what if." That place is dangerous because it leaves you wondering about your potential to accomplish anything in life. Remember that you are the only person that can set a limit on what you can do. There will definitely be individuals who will do their best to keep you from elevating yourself, but use them as you use those old boxes of memories, a step stool to elevate you higher.

It is completely okay for everyone to not understand your journey; they are not supposed to. Do not be surprised that your biggest supporters are those individuals you have yet to meet. Some of your family and friends may be secretly betting against you, but it is okay, that is your motivation to get it done. Do not be afraid to ask for help because you cannot do it all by yourself. Surround yourself with individuals who are strong in your area of weakness. When you do that, it will afford you the time to continue to master your skill and stay in your lane.

I am so thrilled to know that many of you are ready to take action on the steps you have completed in the book. I have prayed that you will be able to hear, receive, and grow by what you have read in this book. Do not keep all of this great knowledge to yourself. The blessing is in helping someone else.

In the upcoming weeks and months you will need to take a step back to self-examine.

Those goals that were once important to you, did you accomplish them?

Have you created the impact that you wanted to achieve at this point in your life?

Does your life work for you or are you just working to make it in life?

What will make you happy?

This is the best chapter of this book because you now have unlocked all of the steps necessary to redesign yourself. You now have the opportunity to design the person you want to be. Remember when you were little and you acted out your dream career? Well we are going to do the same exercise now, but as an adult designing ourselves. How many of you actually became what you told yourself you would become as an child? If you are nodding, I am so proud of you because that means you made a decision early on that you were going to follow-through with your dreams. But how many individuals do you know that followed through with their dreams, but became someone they now dislike. It is okay. The redesign is possible for anyone that is willing to go through the process. You will not find your life set in stone anywhere. You have the ability to drop off your old life and pick-up another one, but I pray this book will help you eliminate going down the paths that will lead to nowhere.

These next steps will act as your compass to guide you to design the best you possible. Now is also a good time to let you know that this process will not happen overnight. It will take some time to really cultivate your vision through logic and planning. When you finally realize the direction you need to go, the light bulb will shine so bright. I remember when this happened for me. I was driving in the car on my way home from work and the vision flashed before me as if it was happening right at that moment. It was extremely overwhelming because the first thing that came to mind was how am I going to do that? I picked up the phone and shared my vision with one of my good girlfriends who I knew I could trust with this vision and she was just as excited as I was. When I hung up, I began to cry because I knew this was way bigger than me and I thought about all of the lives that will be changed with me taking on this assignment. It took me a little over a year to really pull all the pieces together, but to God be the Glory. It came together and you are experiencing the beginning of this amazing journey.

Here is the first question you must ask yourself; what do you want? Allow yourself to explore your deepest desires and do not tell yourself that you do not deserve them. You absolutely deserve to live life to the fullest, but you must design it. When considering what you want, think about all aspects of your life: personal, family, health, professional, career, success, spiritual growth and enjoyment.

Here are a few tips to assist you in provoking your thoughts.

- Why do you want it?
- Do not focus on the things you do not want, but on the things you want.
- It is okay to dream.
- Be creative.
- What legacy would you like to leave behind?
- What is special about you?
- What brings you joy and happiness?
- What are some secret passions and dreams?

Now you may not be able to answer all of these at one time and it is okay. This is truly a thought provoking exercise that should be fun and not stressful. Take your time in answering the questions and add questions that will help you in redesign you?

What would your best life look like?

Before you begin, I need you to shake off any preconceived notions that you cannot have this ideal life. You are going to need to give yourself permission to dream and visualize how your best life would feel. In this exercise we are going to envision five years from now, 10 years, 15 years and then 20 years.

Here are a few prompts to get you started:

- How will you feel about yourself?
- What have you already accomplished?
- What kind of individuals are in your circle?
- Where do you live?
- Are you happy?
- What do you look like?

So, now that your mind is thinking about these questions, I would like you to close your eyes and see yourself acting out your answers from the above questions. Give yourself as long as you need to complete this, you need this more than you think. Oh, do not think or worry about how you are going to get there. Go ahead close your eyes and dream.

Now that you have dreamt and fantasized about your redesign. You must take some time out daily to go back to that place in your mind. The more you dream about it, the more you began to attract those things that will bring your dream to fruition.

Now, let us begin to put somethings in place to plan out where you want to go. What important actions must you do first to put your dream into motion?

_____
_____
_____

What habits do you need to change or cultivate?

_____
_____
_____

What are some things you think you would need to learn?

_____
_____
_____

Who's on the list to be your support system?

_____
_____
_____

What are the milestones you need to reach along the way?

_____
_____
_____

Whew- you made it! Now you need to decide what to do first. This process may seem overwhelming, but believe me it is worth it. You should feel great about designing the new you. There will be some things that may change and that is great because during the process you will continue to stretch yourself and where you are today is not where you will be months from now. Write the vision and make it plain to redesign the best you.

Redesign the best life for you.

Isaiah 1:19

"If ye be willing and obedient, ye shall eat the good of the land:"

Can You?

Breathe Bonus

YOU ARE WORTH IT

Your life is worth finding. Have you ever been to a funeral and you began to wonder when it is your time, what will they say about you? Will the church be filled with individuals whose lives you have touched and served? Will there be so many testimonies that they have to stop individuals from coming forward? Do not allow your life to end without finding your purpose. Do you realize that the gift that has been placed in you is not for you? That gift inside you is to bless others and the generations that come behind you. Do you know that you are given three-to-four ideas a year that you can act on, but do you realize that most individuals will not act on them because they begin to kill them with their own self-talk. Can you imagine it? Just take the leap of faith. You have to fight for your dreams. Do not be a spectator in life, get in there and fight for what is yours.

I walked away from a six-figure income that most would say was a "good government job" because I was comfortable and the job was no longer serving any purpose in my life. Yes, the money was paying the bills, but I was no longer growing. I knew it was time to go, when I had to literally sit in my car and pray before going into the building and then praying again as I rode the elevator to my floor. It seemed like the more I prayed the worse it got. I walked around the building saying I was "Awesome" so much, I began to have other individuals saying it too. Although, I did not feel awesome while I was there, I had to constantly talk to myself and remind myself that regardless of what happened, what was said, I was AWESOME. That attitude caused me to not complain, oh believe me I would vent to my accountability partner, but never complained. I began to realize where my discomfort was coming from, it was because God had spoken to me at the end of 2015 to put in my letter of resignation in on January 4th, 2016. Guess what? I did not listen. I allowed others to tell me to hang in there and the fear of not having that income coming in began to paralyze me. I began to question the Lord about why he was allowing me to go through what I was going through and he asked me a simple question, "did you do what I instructed you to do? " At that moment, it did not matter what anyone else had to say about my decision. I had to do what God instructed me to do. There are things in your life that God has been speaking to you about, but you have justified why you need to keep it. LET IT GO!!! Now let me be clear, I am not saying that you need to leave your job. You have to seek God as to those things He has instructed you to let go. It could be friends, relationships, habits; whatever it is, TRUST HIM! This is all part of your redesign.

Now, let me ask you a simple question. How much time do you spend working on your goals and dreams? Do you spend as much time working on you yourself as you do watching TV, being on social media or gossiping as you do reading a book, self-reflection or praying? How often do you just sit in a quiet room and think about where you are going and what you want out of life? I ask these questions because it does not matter how many times you read this book or complete the assignments, you will only get out of life what you are willing to sacrifice and put into it. So, I ask you what is your sacrifice to get what you want out of life? What are those things that you are temporarily ready to give up for the long-term gain? I say temporarily because once you have achieved what you were seeking, you will have the time to do all the things you enjoy doing.

What new skill have you acquired? What new investments have you made in you? Set weekly goals and review your progress, build your library by reading good books and attend seminars/conferences that are related to your goals. Make a conscious effort to develop you. Do not let fear stop you from living your dreams. Fear kills dreams and hopes. Fear can do one or two things it can either paralyze you or motivate you.

FEAR

False

Evidence

Appearing

Real

Turn it off. Listen to and read things that will inspire and push you to keep pressing towards your mark.

Philippians 3:14

"I press toward the mark for the prize of the high calling of God in Christ Jesus."

The TEST, The TRIALS, The TEARS!

It is worth it, you are worth it!

Conclusion

I made a promise to myself that I would finish this book on a certain day and that mission was not accomplished. My set completion date was on March 25, 2016. What is the significance in that day? It was Good Friday. What better way to show my love and appreciation for my Heavenly Father and say thank you than by sharing my gift with the world. Because of His love for me He carried and died on His cross. Now that is TRUE LOVE. Guess what? I did not finish my book on that day, but it was okay because I did not allow that to deter me. God orders our steps and everything happens for a reason. You might not know what that reason is, but just know it did not happen because it was not supposed to. As you read through this book, I hope it clarified for you who you are, whose you are and how to love yourself. I have had individuals say "everyone is writing a book these days or what can you help me with." All of the negative comments pushed me even harder to get it done. It took me four months to complete my book, but it was not until I set the date and let God be my pencil.

Have you ever allowed the opinion of someone else to stop you from doing what you know you are supposed to do? I know that I have. There have been many times I allowed someone else's opinion of what I should do to stop me from reaching my goal. If you know that you have prayed and God has spoken to you regarding your situation. Do it! It may not always be appealing to others around you regarding your decisions and that is okay. They do not have a heaven nor a hell to put you in. I am no longer a slave to what others think and neither should you. To God be the glory. I have been faced with major distractions in my life and I allowed those distractions to cause me to lose my focus. What I had to realize is that distractions will always be there, but it only matters how you deal with them. When I chose not to allow excuses to cripple me from birthing what God placed in me, that was all the motivation I needed. I had something to say and I pray that it has helped you in your journey to a better you. Remember that as long as you move forward every day, you are closer to achieving your goal. My five-year old said something that ignited a fire deep down in my soul… "Practice makes progress." Keep striving, keep loving, keep pressing towards your mark because you are worth it!

My eye gate is shielded; my ear gate is plugged. I am ready for whatever comes my way and I will, no matter what, keep pressing towards my mark because I am worth fighting for.

You were worth dying for! – Jesus

Epilogue

Wow! When I began to look back over my life and some of the decisions I made, I realized that each test, each trial, each tear was meant to grow my faith and me. There were times when I smiled so much that I even fooled myself, but I was miserable. I kept wondering, Lord what is it that you would have me to do. That was my prayer and it was constantly on my mind. The more I began to question my purpose, the more wisdom I received, those things that used to push my buttons, no longer send me over the edge. When I began to have a greater relationship with my Heavenly Father, the more in touch I became with why He put me on this earth and how He wanted me to serve His individuals.

When you know what you know, you do not have to try to please anyone. You realize that you are enough and those bags they are trying to drop off at your door; they will began to realize that you are not picking them up anymore. Why? Because you have moved. Your drop-off facility has closed and if there are any attempts to leave a package, it will be stamped "return to sender."

I am so in love with who I have become and what is getting ready to happen in the future…Love yourself, love your life and love the journey.

www.ingramcontent.com/pod-product-compliance
Lightning Source LLC
Chambersburg PA
CBHW070949180426
43194CB00041B/1997